Pen & Postcards

A Creative Workbook for Young Letter Writers

INCLUDES TEAR-OUT STATIONERY AND POSTCARDS!

THIS BOOK BELONGS TO:

Pen Pals and Postcards: A Creative Workbook for Young Letter Writers

Written by Renata Paolercio
Design and Illustrations by Erin Gennow, Contributing Illustrations by Olivia Cox

© Modern Kid Press All rights reserved. No part of this publication may be reproduced, distributed, or transmitted, in any form or by any means, including photocopying, recording, or other electronic or mechanical methods, without prior written permission of the publisher, except in the case of brief quotations embodied in critical reviews and certain other noncommercial uses permitted by copyright law.

TABLE OF CONTENTS

Letter to Caregiver	4
Why Write Letters	6
Who Will You Write	7
When Should You Write a Letter	8
Letter Tracker	9
How to Write a Letter	12
Addressing an Envelope	14
My Address Page	15
Address Book	16
Writing a Postcard	22
Postcard Decorating Ideas	24
Stationery Pages	28
Additional Resources	69
Postcards	71

DEAR CAREGIVER,

Thank you for picking up a copy of *Pen Pals & Postcards: A Creative Workbook for Young Letter Writers*! I was inspired to create this book with my daughter, Olivia, as I watched her develop a passion for drawing. Making original birthday cards and handmade gifts fostered a genuine level of creativity and thoughtful intention between us. Together we wanted to pass along an interactive book that might inspire other children and caregivers to do the same, while teaching children the importance of written communication.

We view this journey as two-fold:
1. spreading kindness through thoughtful communications and
2. developing a sense of confidence and creativity in one's ability to communicate with writing tools and paper.

Sending postcards to friends and families is a gift in and of itself. It is extra exciting when it yields its own return in the form of a written reply. Whether your child chooses to use Olivia's designs as inspiration or create their own original ones, the recipient of their thoughts and creativity will be pleasantly surprised.

If you are supporting a very young child on this journey, remember that our early writers and learners can begin this journey with simple forms that do not have to be complete drawings. Even just a word or scribble can carry a great deal of meaning and be treasured by loved ones near and far. Help them place their first stamp and encourage them to observe while watching you write out the address. This can be a family learning experience that encourages and inspires our writers of the future!

We hope you and your child enjoy embarking upon this journey as much as we enjoyed creating it! Happy corresponding!

— RENATA, OLIVIA, AND PAOLO

WHY WRITE LETTERS?

Have you ever received a postcard in the mail? Were you excited to hear that something in that big pile of letters, magazines, and envelopes was actually for YOU? Writing a postcard or letter to someone is a surprise gift that brightens someone's day. Whether you write a simple hello, a special seasonal greeting, or share some news, receiving a postcard or letter is something that people have enjoyed doing for hundreds of years.

Before phones, computers, airplanes, televisions, cars, and any form of transportation existed, letters were the only way to share ideas and feelings with another person when you weren't with them.

FUN FACT!
The first letter can be traced back to 500 BC!

WHO WILL YOU WRITE TO?

The fun thing about sending and receiving mail is that you can write to a friend that lives 10 minutes away, 10 miles away or 1,000 miles away. Sometimes even when people live close to us, we don't have a chance to connect with them as often as we'd like to. So drop a line to a new friend, an old friend, a grandparent, a cousin or a penpal. It is always a good time to put pen to paper and share your thoughts.

WHAT'S A PENPAL?

Someone you get to know through exchanging letters.

WHEN SHOULD YOU WRITE LETTERS?

People write letters for many reasons. One may write a letter to inform someone of an event that will or has happened. Today, many people write letters to share in celebrations of holidays and other special days. Below are some fun holidays when you could write and send a letter.

- Birthdays
- New Years
- Valentine's Day
- St. Patrick's Day
- April Fools Day
- Mothers Day
- Father's Day
- Grandparents Day
- Junteenth
- July 4th
- End of Summer

- Back to School
- Halloween
- Thanksgiving
- Diwali
- Christmas
- Kwanza
- Hanukkah
- Other
- _____
- _____
- _____

LETTER TRACKER

Use these pages to keep track of letters you send and receive.

Date: _____
To: _____

Date: _____
From: _____

Date: _____
To: _____

Date: _____
From: _____

Date: _____
To: _____

Date: _____
From: _____

Date: _____
To: _____

Date: _____
From: _____

Date: _____
To: _____

Date: _____
From: _____

Date: _____
To: _____

Date: _____
From: _____

LETTER TRACKER

Date: _____
To: _____

Date: _____
From: _____

Date: _____
To: _____

Date: _____
From: _____

Date: _____
To: _____

Date: _____
From: _____

Date: _____
To: _____

Date: _____
From: _____

Date: _____
To: _____

Date: _____
From: _____

Date: _____
To: _____

Date: _____
From: _____

LETTER TRACKER

Date: _____
To: _____

Date: _____
From: _____

Date: _____
To: _____

Date: _____
From: _____

Date: _____
To: _____

Date: _____
From: _____

Date: _____
To: _____

Date: _____
From: _____

Date: _____
To: _____

Date: _____
From: _____

Date: _____
To: _____

Date: _____
From: _____

HOW DO YOU WRITE A LETTER?

DATE
When writing a letter put the date on the upper left or right hand side of your paper.

SALUTATION
Then, skip a line, and starting on the left hand side of the paper, write your salutation (greeting). This greeting addresses the person for whom you are writing. An example of a salutation is, Dear Grandpa.

BODY
After the salutation skip another line and start the body of your letter. This includes the main ideas you will tell your recipient.

CLOSING
Following the body of the letter skip another line and write your closing. The closing is a way of completing your letter by saying, Thank You, With Love, Kind Regards, etc. Capitalize your closing and follow it with a comma.

SIGNATURE
Finally add your signature, which means to sign your name. This is traditionally done by hand with a pencil or pen.

SALUTATION

DATE

February 1, 2025

Dear Auntie,

BODY

    I hope you are well. Today at school we had art class. I painted hearts on pink paper. It was so much fun!

    I miss you. I can't wait to see you on Valentine's Day.

CLOSING

Love,

Sally

SIGNATURE

ADDRESSING AN ENVELOPE

ENVELOPE FRONT

POSTAGE STAMP

Mail requires a postage stamp in order to send it from one place to another. It is a form of money, a way to pay for the letter to be sent and delivered.

RECIPIENT'S ADDRESS

The address of who and where the letter is going, so the mail person can deliver it to the correct place.

ENVELOPE BACK

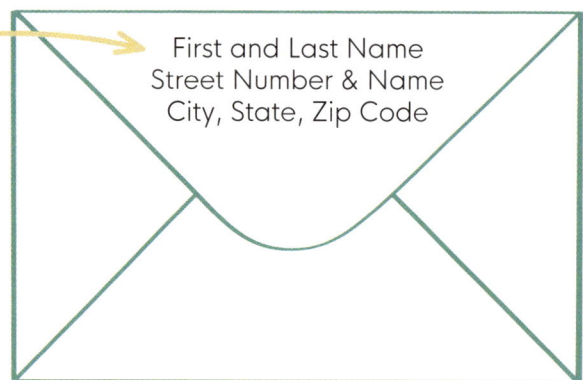

RETURN ADDRESS

The return address is the address of the sender. If a letter cannot be sent or is lost it can be sent back to the sender.

MY ADDRESS PAGE

Practice writing your street address 4 times on the lines below. An address includes the name of the person, the house or building number, the street name, city, state abbreviation, and zip code.

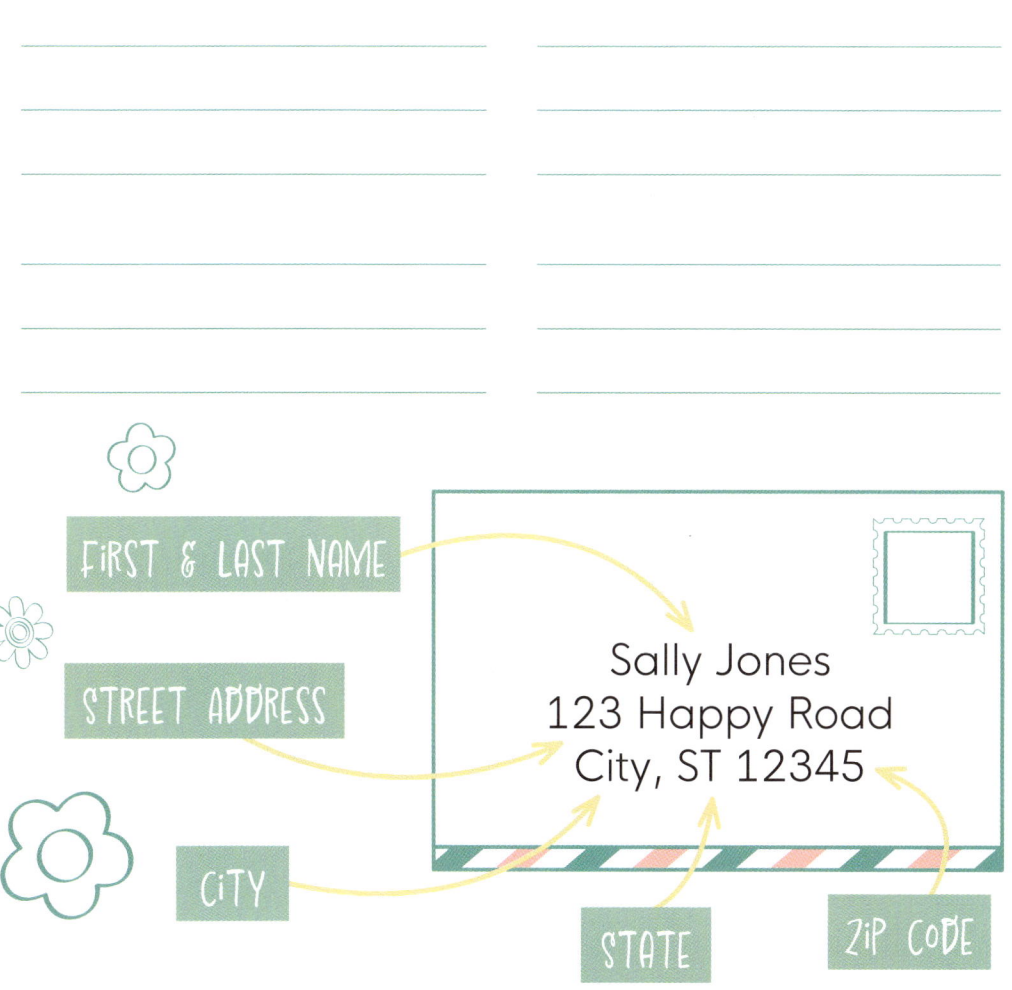

ADDRESS BOOK

Here's a place to write down addresses and birthdays of friends and family so you always have them handy when you would like to write a letter.

Name:
Birthday:
Address:
Notes:

Name:
Birthday:
Address:
Notes:

Name:
Birthday:
Address:
Notes:

Name:
Birthday:
Address:
Notes:

Name:

Birthday:

Address:

Notes:

Name:

Birthday:

Address:

Notes:

Name:

Birthday:

Address:

Notes:

Name:

Birthday:

Address:

Notes:

Name:

Birthday:

Address:

Notes:

Name: _____
Birthday: _____
Address: _____
Notes: _____

Name: _____
Birthday: _____
Address: _____
Notes: _____

Name: _____
Birthday: _____
Address: _____
Notes: _____

Name: _____
Birthday: _____
Address: _____
Notes: _____

Name: _____
Birthday: _____
Address: _____
Notes: _____

Name:
Birthday:
Address:
Notes:

Name:
Birthday:
Address:
Notes:

Name:
Birthday:
Address:
Notes:

Name:
Birthday:
Address:
Notes:

Name:
Birthday:
Address:
Notes:

Name:
Birthday:
Address:
Notes:

Name:
Birthday:
Address:
Notes:

Name:
Birthday:
Address:
Notes:

Name:
Birthday:
Address:
Notes:

Name:
Birthday:
Address:
Notes:

Name: _____
Birthday: _____
Address: _____
Notes: _____

Name: _____
Birthday: _____
Address: _____
Notes: _____

Name: _____
Birthday: _____
Address: _____
Notes: _____

Name: _____
Birthday: _____
Address: _____
Notes: _____

Name: _____
Birthday: _____
Address: _____
Notes: _____

WRITING A POSTCARD

A postcard is a flat card with an image on the front and space on the back to write the message, address the recipient, and place the stamp. It is typically mailed without an envelope.

Because a postcard is lighter than a letter in an envelope and flat, the postage stamp costs less than a stamp required for a letter in an envelope.

POSTCARD FRONT

You can create your own amazing arwork!

POSTCARD BACK

DATE

SALUTATION

STAMP

September 1, 2025

Dear Grandpa,
    I had an amazing first day of school! I can't wait to tell you about it when you visit next month.
    Love,
    Harper

John Johnson
123 Happy St.
Juno, AK
99850

BODY

CLOSING & SIGNATURE

RECIPIENT'S NAME & ADDRESS

MONTHLY POSTCARD IDEAS

JANUARY

FEBRUARY

MARCH

APRIL

MAY

JUNE

Check out this original artwork from Olivia and use it as inspiration for your own postcards on pages 71-82.

JULY

AUGUST

SEPTEMBER

OCTOBER

NOVEMBER

DECEMBER

LETTER WRITING IDEAS

 **January**: It's a New Year! Start the year off by writing a letter to someone you recently met and want to connect with more often, or someone you haven't seen or spoken to in a while with whom you would like to reconnect!

 February: It's that time of year...when we tell someone how much we care about them. Who will you choose to say Happy Valentine's Day to? *I love you Grandma! Can't wait to come visit again. I miss you my friend! Seeing you over break was so much fun! Hey cousin! Let's start some letter writing so we can stay in touch! I love you!*

 **March**: Do you know anyone who is Irish and celebrates St. Patrick's Day? Many people aren't Irish but still enjoy wearing green and eating Irish soda bread or enjoying an Irish dish like Shepard's pie on March 17th. Drop a line to a friend or someone you know that enjoys such traditions!

 April: Have you decorated eggs this month? Gone to any egg hunts and met that big furry guy that gives out chocolate treats? Check in with a friend to find out what kind of Spring activities they've enjoyed this month. *Did you remember April fool's day this year? Share a good joke with a friend or tell them something funny you or someone you know did on April 1st!*

May: Happy Mother's Day! So many people to whom we can send good wishes this month: an Aunt, a teacher, a friend, a Grandmother and of course...your own Mom!

 **June**: Summer is on the horizon! Drop a line to a friend and see what fun plans they have in the works.

 **July**: Temperatures are rising, camps are in full swing and everyone is enjoying different activities outside of the school year. Check in with someone to say hello and tell them what you are doing this month!

 August: With back to school around the corner, it's a perfect time to tell someone how your summer went!

 September: Wish someone a "happy first day back at school!" and let them know how yours went.

 **October**: BOO! Share your costume plans with a friend, or simply say, "HAPPY HALLOWEEN!"

 November: GRATITUDE is in the air as we gear up for this fun holiday. Tell someone you are thinking of them during this time or that you are happy to have them in your life.

 **December**: 'Tis the season to eat treats, exchange presents, and be jolly! Wish someone a happy holiday season!

STATIONERY PAGES

Use the following stationery pages to write your own letters to friends and family. There are both lined and unlined pages to write on, decorate, and color. Some of the pages have fun themes for holidays and birthdays. Cut out the pages when you're ready to send a letter. Get creative and have fun!

WHAT DOES STATIONERY MEAN?
Writing paper, often with matching envelopes.

ADDITIONAL RESOURCES

Please scan this QR code for additional activities!

PRINTABLE ENVELOPE TEMPLATE!

A SPECIAL SONG!

POP-UP CARD TUTORIAL!

Place Stamp Here

To:

© Modern Kid Press

Place Stamp Here

To:

© Modern Kid Press

Place Stamp Here

To:
_____
_____
_____
_____

© Modern Kid Press

Place Stamp Here

To:
_____
_____
_____
_____

© Modern Kid Press

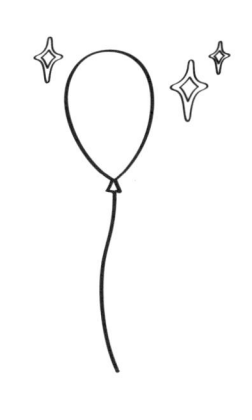

Place Stamp Here

To:

© Modern Kid Press

Place Stamp Here

To:

© Modern Kid Press

Place Stamp Here

To:
_____
_____
_____
_____

© Modern Kid Press

Place Stamp Here

To:
_____
_____
_____
_____

© Modern Kid Press

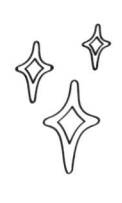

Place Stamp Here

To:

© Modern Kid Press

Place Stamp Here

To:

© Modern Kid Press

HELLO SUNSHINE

BEST FRIENDS

Place Stamp Here

To:

© Modern Kid Press

Place Stamp Here

To:

© Modern Kid Press

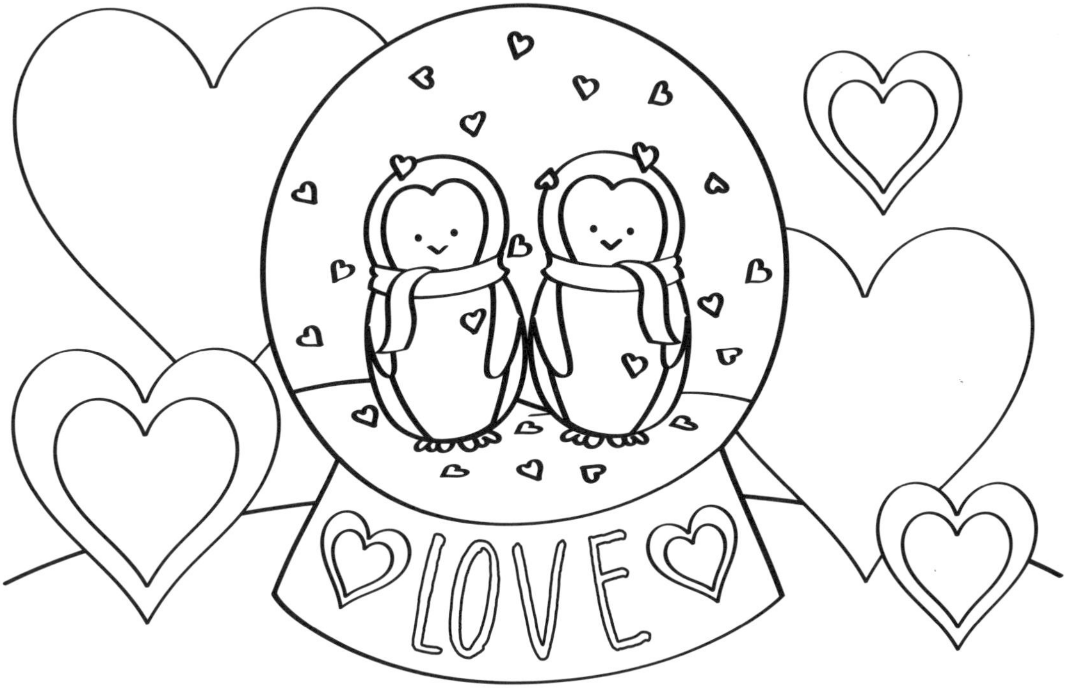
LOVE

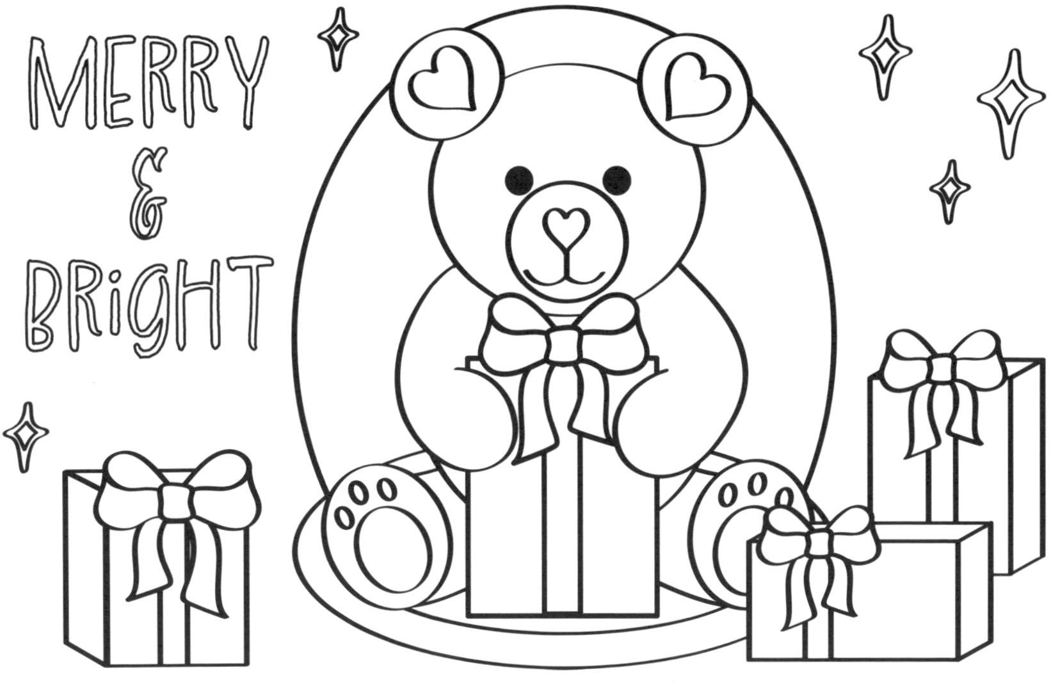
MERRY
&
BRiGHT

Place Stamp Here

To:

© Modern Kid Press

Place Stamp Here

To:

© Modern Kid Press